WISCONSIN

A Turner Educational Services, Inc. book. Based on the Portrait of America television series created by R.E. (Ted) Turner.

Library of Congress Number: 85-12176

1234567890   908988878685

Library of Congress Cataloging in Publication Data

Thompson, Kathleen.
  Wisconsin.

  (Portrait of America)
  "A Turner book."
  Summary: Discusses the history, economy, culture, and future of Wisconsin. Also includes a state chronology, pertinent statistics, and maps.
  1. Wisconsin—Juvenile literature. [1. Wisconsin] I. Title. II. Series: Thompson, Kathleen. Portrait of America.
F581.3.T46   1985   977.5   85-12176
ISBN 0-86514-448-6 (lib. bdg.)
ISBN 0-86514-523-7 (softcover)

Cover Photo: © 1980, Eric Oxendorf

Portrait of AMERICA

WISCONSIN

Kathleen Thompson

Photographs from Portrait of America programs
courtesy of Turner Program Services, Inc.

A TURNER BOOK
RAINTREE PUBLISHERS

CONTENTS

Introduction

Wisconsin, the Badger State.

"It took me some time to realize that there is no better area in the world than this neck of the woods. . . ."

Wisconsin: cows, combines, cows, beer, cows, forests, fishing, factories, and cows.

"On the whole, Milwaukee is a pretty sturdy place."

"We still have the finest, cleanest lake in the world. It's crystal clear. You can look down and see the bottom."

"As far back as I can remember, way back in grade school, they've told us we've got a hungry, hungry world to feed."

From the mountains of Switzerland, from Scandinavia and Germany, immigrants came to the cold, clear, wooded land of Wisconsin. They brought with them their skill with cattle, their talent for making cheese and other fine dairy products.

They also brought a practical, open spirit that was to make Wisconsin one of the most politically progressive states in our nation.

Like the handicrafts of its people, the state of Wisconsin is clean, pretty, and . . . solid.

An ethnic dance festival in Milwaukee.

Fox, French, and La Follette

They kept trying to get to China. Columbus was looking for China and found the West Indies. Jean Nicolet was looking for China and found Wisconsin.

To begin with, the explorers didn't know that there was anything between Europe and their cherished goal—the riches of the Orient. Then, they just couldn't believe how *much* there was. If they just kept looking, they were sure, they could find a way to sail west to the land described by Marco Polo.

French explorer Jean Nicolet was looking for that legendary water route to China when he stepped onto the shore of Green Bay in 1634. He was greeted, not by the Chinese emperor, but by Winnebago Indians. The Winnebago, of

The Wisconsin shoreline, near Green Bay.

course, had no idea what this strange man expected. But *they* certainly didn't expect him.

For centuries, the Winnebago, Dakota, and Menominee Indians had lived and farmed in the area we now call Wisconsin. They had a stable sort of existence based on farming, hunting, and fishing. With great skill, they built comfortable wooden homes, sewed leather and fur clothing as protection against the cold winters. Their land was fertile and their life was prosperous.

When Nicolet reported back to France that his search for the Northwest Passage had yielded nothing but more of America, Europe lost interest in the area for a while. There was already so much of America to deal with. But about twenty-five years later, French fur traders came into Wisconsin. They were soon followed by Father René Ménard, who set up a Roman Catholic mission. Other missionaries, traders, and explorers followed.

In most areas where the French explored there were good relations between Europeans and

State Historical Society of Wisconsin

Indians. Wisconsin was no exception, for a while. The French who came in were usually not settlers. They didn't take away Indian lands to make farms and towns. They either hunted and trapped side by side with the Indians or traded European goods for the skins the Indians brought them.

Then, in 1712, this peaceful relationship came to an end. The French tried to take control of the Fox and Wisconsin rivers. The Fox Indians were one of the groups that had entered Wisconsin during the 1600s. Others were the Chippewa, the Sauk, the Ottawa, the Kickapoo, the Huron, the Miami, the Illinois, and the Potawatomi. Many had been driven from lands farther east by Europeans. Some had come to get away from other Indian wars.

The Fox Indians fought the French for control of the rivers for twenty-eight years. The French won, in a way. They defeated the Fox, but they lost forever their friendly relations

This early twentieth-century painting depicts the French explorer Jean Nicolet landing among the Winnebago Indians in Green Bay in 1634.

with the Indians of the area. They also lost a lot of men they couldn't afford to lose in that area.

At this time, France and Britain were struggling for control of the new continent. The French and Indian War was the turning point in that struggle. When the British won in 1763, France gave up its claims to most of America. The Wisconsin area, among others, became British.

French fur traders stayed in Wisconsin. There were still few settlers from any country in the area.

After the Revolutionary War, Wisconsin became part of the United States. But the British didn't actually leave until after the War of 1812. In the meantime, Wisconsin was first part of the Northwest Territory, then Indiana Territory, then Illinois Territory, then Michigan Territory.

And still, there weren't many settlers in the area. It was a place Americans were satisfied with leaving to the Indians—until 1822.

In 1822, it was discovered that the land of Wisconsin was rich in lead. By 1827, the area where

At the left is an 1839 drawing of a cross section of a lead mine. Above is a present-day photograph of Mineral Point—one of the areas where lead was discovered.

lead had been found was no longer Indian land. And the rush of settlers into Wisconsin had begun.

Not all the miners were year-round residents. During the cold winters, many of them went back south. They were nick-named "suckers" after a Mississippi River fish that goes south for the winter. Other miners dug caves and stayed in them during the winter. They were called "badgers." That nickname stuck with the state.

Wisconsin saw part of the

Black Hawk War. Sauk Indians who had been forced to move from Illinois to Iowa marched back into their homeland but finally retreated into Wisconsin, where they were defeated in 1832.

The Territory of Wisconsin was formed in 1836. At the time, there were about 12,000 people living within the boundaries of the present state. Most of them were in the region where lead had been found. Twelve years later, Wisconsin became a state. By 1850, there were more than 300,000 people living in Wisconsin.

In the early years of the state, the biggest problem was transportation. There were steamboats and sailing ships on the Mississippi River and the Great Lakes, but that didn't help the farmers inland. There was no solution until the railroad came into the state in the 1850s. By that time, the whole country was in the grips of a much bigger problem.

Most of Wisconsin's population were against slavery. In 1854, the Kansas-Nebraska Bill was introduced in Congress to allow these two new territories to decide for themselves on the question of slavery. A protest meeting was held in Ripon, Wisconsin, that led to the formation of the Republican Party.

In 1860, that party's candidate for president, Abraham Lincoln, won the election. Within a year, the Civil War had begun. Wisconsin sent more than 90,000 soldiers into the Union army. The state also contributed about one hundred million bushels of wheat.

On October 8, 1971, the Great Chicago Fire destroyed most of that city, killing about 300 people. On the same night, fire struck northeastern Wisconsin. The great Peshtigo forest fire spread into Michigan and, before it was over, 1,200 people had lost their lives.

13

Robert La Follette (above) is shown campaigning for president in 1924. Contributors to his campaign received certificates like the one shown above, right.

Since the beginnings of the Republican Party, Wisconsin had been a Republican state. In the late 1890s there was a split in the party. In 1900, the Progressive wing put its leader, Robert

M. La Follette, Sr., in the governor's mansion.

"Battling Bob" La Follette led a fight for social and economic reform in the state. He was the first of a long line of Wisconsin politicians who proved that the people of Wisconsin would welcome changes more daring than most of the country could even think about.

La Follette came up with the "Wisconsin Idea." His theory was that government should use the best minds available to it to serve the people. He set up a "brain trust." It included professors from the University of Wisconsin and other universities— all experts in economics, politics, and administration.

The results were far in advance of most of the rest of the country. Before World War I, Wisconsin had adopted an inheritance tax, pensions for teachers, a workers' compensation law, a minimum wage law for women and children, and a pension plan for mothers.

The Progressives lost control of the state in 1915, and the old-school Republicans led Wisconsin through World War I. But in 1921, the Progressives came back. And in that year, Wisconsin gave women complete civil and property rights.

"Battling Bob" La Follette ran for President of the United States in 1924 and received almost five million votes. In 1925, he died. His son, Robert, Jr., was elected to the Senate seat his father had held, and he served in the Senate for twenty-one years.

In 1930, another La Follette was elected governor of Wisconsin. This was Robert's younger son, Philip. He lost the 1932 election but was reelected in 1934 and 1936. In 1934, he and his followers withdrew from the Republican Party and formed the Progressive Party. During the La Follettes' time in office,

Wisconsin passed the most progressive labor laws in the country. The state had the first unemployment compensation law. The legislature also passed measures to help farmers pay their debts.

In 1938, the Progressives lost to the old-style Republicans and the new governor did away with many of the agencies the Progressives had set up. But the years when the La Follettes and their party led Wisconsin were a historic time for this midwestern state.

This building—originally a schoolhouse—was where the Republican Party was founded in 1854.

Doug Lyke, Ripon Community Printers

After World War II, the whole country saw a rise in manufacturing. Agriculture became less important to the economies of most states, including Wisconsin.

Wisconsin had become a major dairy state. It still is today. But in the 1950s and 1960s, Americans began to watch their weight and count their calories. The demand for dairy products fell. In 1951, there were 132,000 dairy farms in Wisconsin. By 1969, there were fewer than half that many. New farm machinery meant that fewer farm workers were needed. People began to move into the cities to work in factories.

This clock, in Milwaukee, is the largest four-sided clock in the world. Below is the Port of Milwaukee.

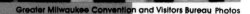

Shown above (in the tan coat) is Vince Lombardi, who was the coach of the Green Bay Packers football team.

After the Progressives, politics in Wisconsin became more conservative. In the 1950s, a Wisconsin senator named Joseph R. McCarthy became known across the country and around the world by accusing everyone from Hollywood screenwriters to President Dwight D. Eisenhower of being ''soft on Communism.''

In the 1960s, the St. Lawrence Seaway began to bring ocean-going ships to ports in Wisconsin. The state lost the Milwaukee Braves to Atlanta but got to cheer the Green Bay Packers to victory.

In the 1970s and 1980s, manufacturing continued to expand and Milwaukee got a new baseball team.

It's still not China, but today Wisconsin is a state with a unique history of political openness, special charm, serene beauty, and an informed and interested population. As you look around Wisconsin, you get the feeling that this state is just what its people intended it to be.

National Park Service

Portrait of America

By the Shores
of Gitchee Gumee

"There was no other area like this. And there was talk even to the point that if they would attempt to effect a removal, that the people would rather die than remove."

In the history of America, it's great to find a place where the Indians won. Around Bayfield, there is such a place.

Henry Buffalo is a Chippewa Indian. His people have lived on the shore of Lake Superior for centuries. They called it Gitchee Gumee. They fished the lake and it provided their living and their way of life. They still fish here. But there was a time when the United States government wanted to take their land away.

The year was 1850. All across the country, government troops were forcing Indian tribes off their lands. The *Trail of Tears* saw seventy thousand men, women, and children pushed out of the southeastern United States to a dry, flat land called Oklahoma.

Henry Buffalo's great-great-grandfather, Chief Buffalo, knew that moving would destroy his people. So, at the age of eighty, he made the long journey to Washington, D.C., to talk to President Fillmore.

"He stated that he wanted a reserve that would follow the coast all the way around to Sand River, and that was approximately seventy-eight hundred acres."

Henry Buffalo is shown against the background of a setting sun and the Lake Superior shoreline.

19

Chief Buffalo got his reserve. The Chippewa continued to live on the shores of Gitchee Gumee. Then, more than one hundred years later, the Great Lakes states tried to take back the fishing rights that had been guaranteed to the Chippewa.

This time it was the chief's great-great grandson who fought back. He had a law degree from the University of Wisconsin and a copy of his people's treaty with the government. And he won. The Chippewa

kept control of their own fishing.

Today, on Lake Superior, commercial fishing boats are regulated by the United States government. Chippewa boats are regulated by Chippewa tribal law. In some places, this has caused hostility on the part of the commer-

cial boats. But near Bayfield, where Henry Buffalo lives, the two groups work together pretty well.

"There's a real good relationship between the state commercial fishermen and the tribal commercial fishermen, although there is still a lot of competition also between the two."

Without a shot fired or a bow drawn, the Chippewa Indians kept their home and their right to use it.

At the far left is a sculpture of Chief Buffalo. Above is a lighthouse, and at the left are some fishing boats at Bayfield.

Cows, Combines, and Computers

The dairy farms of Wisconsin may be one of the prettiest sights on earth. You can get in a car and drive through gently rolling land with green pastures on either side of you. Dotted along the way are white farmhouses and red barns. A Wisconsin dairy farm looks the way a farm ought to look.

Just past the farms, you may drive through forests of maple, oak, ash, and birch trees. In the fall, their leaves are bright splashes of yellow and red and deep orange. At their feet are purple asters.

As you round a hill, a lake spreads out in front of you, blue as the Wisconsin sky. Families with fishing poles sit along the banks. A slow boat passes in the distance.

Northern Wisconsin in the fall.

Standing at an apple orchard with five kinds of apples piled in bushel baskets around you, it may be hard to think of Wisconsin as a manufacturing state. But it is.

Wisconsin is all that it seems to be. But it's also a lot more.

For a long time, the economy of Wisconsin centered on farming, especially dairy farming. But today, 80 percent of the goods produced in Wisconsin are manufactured products. Of course, many of them are closely tied in with the state's agricultural history.

The largest area of manufacturing in Wisconsin is nonelectric machinery. Factories in the area around Milwaukee make farm equipment and machinery for construction. They make engines, turbines, and machine tools.

The second largest area of manufacturing is even more directly related to farming. Wisconsin makes food products using the farm products of their own state. First among these are dairy products.

Wisconsin cheese factories produce about 40 percent of all

the cheese made in the United States. Wisconsin produces more milk and butter than any other state. Throughout the state, factories make ice cream and dried and evaporated milk. Visiting a cheese factory brings home the fact that manufacturing can really be a part of the world of

Above is one of Wisconsin's many plants that manufacture cheese.

farming. As the large wheels of ripe cheese pass by, you know that you're not all that far from a small dairy farm.

There are also meat packing plants and canneries to process other Wisconsin farm goods.

And there are breweries.

The third largest area of manufacturing relates to the forests, not the farms. Wisconsin is a leader in making paper products, reflecting the fact that half of Wisconsin's land is covered with

forests. Most of those forests were planted after the first growth of trees was cut down. Today, trees are treated like a crop. As one tree is cut down to make cardboard boxes and tissue paper, another is planted to take its place.

Wisconsin factories also make metal products like cans, hardware, knives and forks. Wiscon-

Wisconsin produces more dairy products and sweet corn (right-hand page) than any other state.

sin is one of the leading states in making automobiles and other transportation equipment. And electric and electronic equipment is made in large factories near Milwaukee.

But in a sense, agriculture remains at the heart of Wisconsin. Almost 200,000 people still work on farms here. They are responsible for about 19 percent of the value of goods produced in the state.

Wisconsin has more than 90,000 farms. The largest part of them are dairy farms. Wisconsin has led the country in dairy products for more than seventy years. More than half of the total farm income of the state comes from dairying.

Wisconsin farmers also raise animals for meat. The biggest field crops—corn, oats, and hay— are grown to feed livestock.

Though they account for a smaller percentage of the total farm income, vegetables and fruit are a big part of Wisconsin's farming. Wisconsin produces more beets, green peas, snap beans, and sweet corn than any other state. It's near the top in cabbage, carrots, lima beans, and potatoes.

Wisconsin farmers raise most of the fruits that thrive in more northern climates. They grow apples and cherries and most kinds of berries.

Wisconsin also raises more minks than any other state.

All in all, through agriculture and manufacturing, Wisconsin does its part in feeding the world. It does its part in producing the things that people need. There's something very practical about most of the things that are made in Wisconsin.

And there's something very practical about the people of Wisconsin.

American Dairy Association of Wisconsin

27

Roots in Wisconsin

"My family's been in Wisconsin for four generations . . . since 1864. And I'm still here. So we've been in Wisconsin for a long time."

Joanne Williams is a television reporter. She is also a black citizen of Wisconsin whose roots go back a long way in the state. She knows and loves her city, Milwaukee. In fact, because of her job, she probably knows it better than most people. She believes it's different.

"When you look at even the poor areas of Milwaukee, and you compare it to the poor areas of cities of comparable size, it just doesn't look the same. Even the public housing. The first projects were built as townhouses. Milwaukee is such a clean city, physically clean city, compared to some other places."

And yet, Joanne's job shows her Milwaukee's problems, problems like hypothermia. Hypothermia is a condition in which the temperature of the body falls dangerously low. It happens when people get too cold—old people, for example, who don't have enough money to heat their homes.

Joanne goes out into Milwaukee asking questions and finding out about its problems.

"Well, I'll tell you, we don't have the thermostat over sixty-eight at any time."

"You've had to do some things to make things warmer, right?"

"We've had to do a lot of things to make things warmer, yes."

Every city has its own problems. Milwaukee is no exception. But Joanne Williams sees no reason to leave the state where her family has lived for 120 years. She sees a special quality to life in Wisconsin, life in Milwaukee.

"Milwaukee is such a hometown. It's a place where you come to have your kids and raise your family. For people of all ethnic backgrounds."

At the right is reporter Joanne Williams, and in the background are the Pabst Theater (far right) in downtown Milwaukee and one of Milwaukee's older neighborhoods.

Portrait of America

Portrait of America

Skiing Toward a New Lifestyle

"Right now I believe that we are living the kind of life that we would want our children to live. I think that maybe fifteen years or so ago, we weren't doing that."

The change in Carol Duffy's life came from two sticks of wood—a pair of cross-country skis. Of course, it wasn't the sport itself so much as finding something she loved, something that brought more joy into her life.

"I just put on those skis and I absolutely fell in love with the sport. . . . Sometimes you do a certain thing and you know it's for you and that's the way I felt about it. I sort of talked Tom into—well, three years later we decided we'd ski the long race together and that's what we did."

Carol Duffy is shown against the background of the start of a Birkebeiner.

Carol's husband Tom felt the same way she did about cross-country skiing. And the skiing gave them a new way of looking at the life they were leading. That was the important thing. It made them think about what they wanted out of life and whether they were getting it.

"Well, I think it's changed priorities. Now, skiing is important enough that we make time for the skiing and de-emphasize the importance of making money and working. It's an important change and one that I wish I'd have started earlier in life than I did."

Not far from the Duffys' home, there is a special cross-country skiing event every year. It is called the American Birkebeiner. About seventy-eight hundred skiers come out to race thirty-one miles. The Duffys raced in their first Birkebeiner not long after their eleventh child was born.

There's a special excitement to the race.

"As you get to the starting line, it's much like a group of stallions. They stamp their skis and the music is blaring and it just builds and builds and builds until finally the cannon fires and . . . wow! They're all going."

Every year, Tom and Carol Duffy race in the Birkebeiner. They enjoy the race and the thrill of competition. But the important thing is the skiing. The important thing is the way of life.

At the far right is Tom Duffy. At the right are skiers on the course of a Birkebeiner, and the 1985 winners (above, right).

Ginny Peifer

"I think as you get older all you think about is food and that type of recreation. And we just feel now that the example that we're setting for our children is really good. We're proud of ourselves."

Ginny Pelfer

Portrait of America

Museum of the City of New York

Sons and Daughters of the Middle Border

"Nice town, y'know what I mean? Nobody very remarkable ever come out of it—s'far as we know."

When the stage manager introduces the town of Grover's Corners in the play *Our Town,* he uses these words. They might seem to fit a lot of Wisconsin towns—like Kenosha and Appleton and Sauk City. Walking down their main streets, you might be surprised at exactly how many "very remarkable" people have come out of them.

There's Thornton Wilder himself, the playwright who wrote *Our Town* and the novelist who wrote *The Bridge of San Luis Rey,* both of which won Pulitzer Prizes. He later wrote *The Matchmaker,* which became the musical *Hello, Dolly,* and *The Skin of Our Teeth,* which collected another Pulitzer Prize for him.

Thornton Wilder.

Ringling Bros.—Barnum & Bailey Combined Shows, Inc. (sic)
Circus World Museum of Baraboo, Wisconsin

In the 1920s, it seemed as though every other Pulitzer Prize in literature was going to a Wisconsin writer. In 1922, Zona Gale won the prize in drama for a play based on her novel, *Miss Lulu Bett.* It was a humorously realistic look at the life of a small town spinster. Zona Gale was, in the words of critic Ludwig Lewisohn, "a very tender spirit" who wrote with insight, sympathy, and understanding.

In the same year, Hamlin Gar-

Wisconsin has been the home of many circuses. Below the poster for the "greatest show on earth" is a circus parade in Milwaukee.

The Great Circus Parade

land won the prize in biography for his *A Daughter of the Middle Border*. Garland was an important part of a new wave in realism in American literature with his stories and novels.

Then, in 1925, Edna Ferber took the Pulitzer for her novel *So Big*. She would also contribute to classics like the play *Show Boat* and the novel *Cimarron*.

The Ringling Brothers were born in Wisconsin. The great magician and escape artist Harry Houdini was raised in Appleton. Orson Welles started here and went on to terrify the country with his radio broadcast "The War of the Worlds" and to bring new life to film with his movie *Citizen Kane*. Alfred Lunt was born in Wisconsin, moved to New York where he met Lynn Fontanne, and became one half of the greatest acting couple in the history of the American stage.

This is a photograph of the Ringling family taken in 1894.

The photograph above shows Frank Lloyd Wright (on the far right) at the construction site of the Johnson Wax buildings, which he designed. At the top are two views of Johnson Wax, which is in Racine.

The list of remarkable people from the towns of Wisconsin goes on to include architect Frank Lloyd Wright, who changed forever the way American cities look. Georgia O'Keeffe brought a stark sensuality to American painting. Thorstein Veblen's *Theory of the Leisure Class* gave us a new way of seeing modern culture.

George F. Kennan is perhaps a classic example of the kind of person Wisconsin has contributed to our society. He was an explorer and journalist who became one of our foremost experts on modern Russia. He combined a sharp intelligence and sophistication with a strong sense of balance. Kennan won the Pulitzer Prize twice, once for his book *Russia Leaves the War*, in 1957, and once for his *Memoirs*, in 1968.

It's difficult to say exactly what it is about Wisconsin that produces this kind of quality in its artists and writers. There's a respect for intelligence and education. There's a foundation in traditional values and a willingness to consider the new.

It may have something to do with those early settlers and the cold winters and leaders like Robert La Follette. It may have something to do with knowing that when something has to be done . . . you do it.

The photograph above is a Greek church, designed by Frank Lloyd Wright, in Milwaukee. The top photograph is a room in Wright's own house in Arizona.

Down on the Farm

"Running a farm is a seven-day-a-week, twenty-four-hour-a-day job. If you have a cow that's going to freshen at one o'clock in the morning, you get up at one o'clock in the morning and you check on it. And if there's field work that has to be done before the weather gets bad, you've got to do that before anything else. Nothing can come before it."

At the age of fifteen, Lisa Mullen already knows what it takes to run a farm. It comes naturally. She and her family have been on their 320 acre farm near Bloomer for four generations. When the first Mullens were here, there were more cows than people in Wisconsin.

Lisa's father, Don, has encouraged his three daughters to learn to love farming.

"I guess we were anxious to see our children interested in 4-H, interested in showing cattle. To be perfectly frank, it's advertising if we do well. And I'm real pleased that my children are interested in doing it."

The Mullens' daughters do very well indeed at places like the Northern Wisconsin State Fair. They show cattle they have raised themselves, and they tend to walk away with ribbons. But they know that farming is a lot more than the state fair.

There's something very satisfying about knowing that you're

At the far right is Lisa Mullen, and in the background are a cattle show ring at a state fair and a typical Wisconsin farm.

Wisconsin Dept. of Agriculture & Consumer Protection

needed. Doctors and nurses know that feeling. Firefighters know it. And so do farmers. For Don Mullen, it's always been part of his love for farming.

"As far back as I can remember, way back in grade school, they've told us we've got a hungry, hungry world to feed. And I think farmers have gone out and really increased their productivity and become more efficient, and have tried to meet that challenge."

Greater Milwaukee Convention and Visitors Bureau

Portrait of America

On, Wisconsin

Wisconsin is not one of the newest states nor one of the oldest. It joined the Union seventy-two years after the Declaration of Independence and has been a state for just under 140 years.

In that time, Wisconsin has moved steadily forward. It began with a boom, a rush of population caused by the discovery of lead in the land. But it quickly settled into a pattern of steady growth and prosperity. The growth has never been spectacular, but then the setbacks have been few and far between as well.

Wisconsin has only about one and one half times as many people living in it now as it had two years after statehood. The economy has moved smoothly from an agricultural base

The Milwaukee skyline.

to a manufacturing base rooted in agriculture.

At one time, loggers cut down most of Wisconsin's trees. The sole exception was the Menominee Indian reservation. But typically, the people of Wisconsin took a look at the situation—the bare ground where forests once grew—and fixed it. They replanted the trees and regulated the logging industry. And if the people of the state have anything to say about it, that ground will never again be bare.

That's a good example of the way Wisconsin deals with its problems. It seldom lets anything get out of control. If it does, Wisconsin fixes it.

The result is that the quality of life in Wisconsin is not just good, but getting better all the time.

A good way to foresee Wisconsin's future might be to look at some of the "firsts" in its past.

Wisconsin had the first kindergarten, the first library for state legislators, the first unemployment compensation law. It was the first state to adopt the number system for marking highways, and it passed the first

law requiring safety belts in new cars bought in the state.

Wisconsin tends to lead the way in practical, common-sense measures that improve the qual-

This is the Horicon Marsh. The birds are great egrets, which inhabit the marsh from May to October.

ity of life.

There is every reason to believe that Wisconsin will move steadily into the future. And it's worth watching to see what the next first will be. It will probably make a lot of sense.

Wisconsin is a state that works.

Important Historical Events in Wisconsin

1634 The first white person in the Wisconsin area is a French explorer, Jean Nicolet. He lands at Green Bay thinking he has found a water route to China.

1660 Fur traders Pierre Esprit Radisson and Médard Chouart, Sieur des Groseilliers, explore the Lake Superior shore in search of furs. They build a post at Chequamegon Bay.

1661 Father René Ménard is the first missionary to visit the area. He establishes a Roman Catholic mission near Ashland.

1665 Father Claude Jean Allouez sets up several missions.

1673 Louis Joliet and Father Jacques Marquette pass through Wisconsin exploring its waterways.

1712 War breaks out between the French and the Fox Indians. Both want control of the Fox and Wisconsin rivers.

1740 The French defeat the Fox Indians and in doing so lose many Indian allies.

1783 The Treaty of Paris ends the American Revolutionary War, and Great Britain gives Wisconsin to the United States.

1787 Wisconsin becomes part of the Northwest Territory.

1800 Wisconsin is included in part of the Indiana Territory.

1809 Wisconsin forms part of the Illinois Territory.

1814 Fort Shelby is built at Prairie du Chien.

1822 Large-scale lead mining draws miners from all over the region to the Fever River area.

1836 The Wisconsin Territory is created. Madison is the capital, and the governor is Henry Dodge.

1845 Swiss colonists in New Glarus make the first cheese in Wisconsin.

1848 Wisconsin joins the Union on May 29 as the 30th state. The capital is Madison, and the governor is Nelson Dewey.

1854 The Republican Party movement begins in Ripon at a meeting organized to protest the Kansas-Nebraska Act.

1856 The Republican Party becomes a powerful force in Wisconsin as Wisconsin's first Republican governor, Coles Bashford, takes office. The first kindergarten in the U.S. opens at Watertown.

1871 A huge forest fire destroys Peshtigo and nearby villages killing 1,200 people.

1872 The Wisconsin Dairymen's Association is organized by William D. Hoard and others at Watertown.

1900 Robert La Follette leads a progressive faction of the Republican Party and wins the governorship. He is reelected in 1902 and 1904. He is known as "Battling Bob" and makes many important governmental reforms.

1911 The state legislature passes many progressive reform laws. They include the creation of a commission to settle labor disputes and a teacher's pension fund.

1921 Women are given full civil and property rights in Wisconsin.

1924 La Follette runs for the presidency of the United States as a Progressive candidate. He is defeated by Republican Calvin Coolidge.

1925 La Follette dies and his son, Robert, Jr., is elected to fill his senate seat.

1932 Wisconsin passes the first state unemployment compensation act.

1958 Gaylord Nelson is elected as Wisconsin's first Democratic governor.

1959 The St. Lawrence Seaway is finished, making seaports out of Wisconsin's Great Lakes cities.

1961 Wisconsin's Menominee Indians are given freedom from federal control. Their reservation becomes the state's seventy-second county. Wisconsin's first sales tax is passed.

1964 Wisconsin is the first state to have its congressional districts redrawn by its supreme court.

1971 The University of Wisconsin System is created.

Wisconsin Almanac

Nickname. The Badger State.

Capital. Madison.

State Bird. Robin.

State Flower. Wood violet.

State Tree. Sugar maple.

State Motto. Forward.

State Song. On, Wisconsin!

State Abbreviations. Wis. (traditional); WI (postal).

Statehood. May 29, 1848, the 30th state.

Government. Congress: U.S. senators, 2; U.S. representatives, 9. **State Legislature:** senators, 33; representatives, 99. **Counties:** 72.

Area. 56,154 sq. mi. (145,438 sq. km.), 26th in size among the states.

Greatest Distances. north/south, 320 mi. (515 km.); east/west, 295 mi. (475 km.).

Elevation. Highest: Timms Hill, 1,952 ft. (595 m). **Lowest:** 581 ft. (177 m).

Population. 1980 Census: 4,705,335 (6.5% increase over 1970). **Density:** 84 persons per sq. mi. (32 persons per sq. km.). **Distribution:** 64% urban, 36% rural. **1970 Census:** 4,417,821.

Economy. Agriculture: milk, beef cattle, hogs, corn. **Manufacturing:** food products, nonelectric machinery, paper products, fabricated metal products, transportation equipment, electric machinery and equipment. **Mining:** sand, gravel, stone, iron ore.

Places to Visit

Apostle Islands, offshore from Bayfield.
Cave of the Mounds, near Blue Mounds.
Door County, on Door Peninsula.
House of the Rock, north of Dodgeville.

Little Norway, near Mount Horeb.
Old World Wisconsin, near Eagle.
Taliesin, near Spring Green.
The Ice Age National Scientific Reserve.

Annual Events

Ski-jumping tournaments in Middleton and Westby (January-February).

World Championship Snowmobile Derby in Eagle River (January).

Syttende Mai Norwegian Festival in Stoughton and Westby (May).

Summerfest in Milwaukee (June).

Lumberjack World Championship in Hayward (July).

Experimental Aircraft Association Fly-in in Oshkosh (July).

Wisconsin State Fair in West Allis (August).

World Dairy Exposition in Madison (October).

Wisconsin Counties